I0409977

Alabama

Holtville High School
10425 Holtville Road
Deatsville, AL 36022-3066
Phone: (334) 569-3034
Principal: Dr. Jimmy Hull
School District: Elmore County Public Schools

Holy Spirit Regional Catholic School
619 Airport Road SW
Huntsville, AL 35802-4358
Phone: (256) 881-4852
Principal: Mr. James Bell
School District: Diocese of Birmingham
  in Alabama

Ramsay Alternative High School
1800 13th Avenue South
Birmingham, AL 35205-5574
Phone: (205) 231-7000
Principal: Dr. Evelyn Nettles
School District: Birmingham City Schools

W. H. Council Traditional School
751 Wilkinson Street
Mobile, AL 36603-1371
Phone: (251) 221-1139
Principal: Ms. Hattie Alexander
School District: Mobile County Public
  School System

Walnut Grove School
1961 Joe Quick Road
New Market, AL 35761-9751
Phone: (256) 828-4677
Principal: Mrs. Kristy Bell
School District: Madison County Schools

West Jefferson Elementary School
4880 Freewill Drive
Quinton, AL 35130-9121
Phone: (205) 379-5550
Principal: Dr. Brenda Cassady
School District: Jefferson County
  Board of Education

Alaska

Aurora Elementary School
5085 10th Street
JBER, AK 99506-1124
Phone: (907) 742-0300
Principal: Mrs. Debbie Washington
School District: Anchorage School District

Arizona

Chandler Traditional Academy - Liberty Campus
550 North Emmett Drive
Chandler, AZ 85225-4183
Phone: (480) 883-4900
Principal: Dr. Beth Ann Bader
School District: Chandler Unified School District

Francisco Vasquez de Coronado
  Elementary School
2301 North Al Harrison Street
Nogales, AZ 85621-3658
Phone: (520) 377-2855
Principal: Ms. Annette Barber
School District: Nogales Unified School District

Sabino High School
5000 North Bowes Road
Tucson, AZ 85749-9522
Phone: (520) 584-7700
Principal: Mr. Matt Munger
School District: Tucson Unified School District

Arizona (continued)

Xavier College Preparatory Roman
  Catholic High School
4710 N 5th Street
Phoenix, AZ 85012-1738
Phone: (602) 277-3772
Principal: Sister Joan Fitzgerald
School District: Diocese of Phoenix

Arkansas

Bergman Elementary School
P. O. Box 1
Bergman, AR 72615-9998
Phone: (870) 741-6404
Principal: Mrs. Debbie Atkinson

Central Park at Morning Star Elementary School
1400 SW Liberty Avenue
Bentonville, AR 72712-7851
Phone: (479) 696-3200
Principal: Mrs. Stacee Freeman
School District: Bentonville Public Schools

Ellen Smith Elementary School
1601 South Donaghey Street
Conway, AR 72034-8634
Phone: (501) 450-4815
Principal: Mrs. DeLanna Lacy
School District: Conway School District

Immaculate Conception Catholic School
223 South 14th Street
Fort Smith, AR 72901-3806
Phone: (479) 783-6798
Principal: Mrs. Sharon Blentlinger
School District: Catholic Diocese of Little Rock

California

Frank C. Leal Elementary School
12920 Droxford Street
Cerritos, CA 90703-6099
Phone: (562) 229-7880
Principal: Ms. Laura Makely
School District: ABC Unified

George W. Simonds Elementary School
6515 Grapevine Way
San Jose, CA 95120-4020
Phone: (408) 535-6251
Principal: Mrs. Melissa Howell
School District: San Jose Unified

James S. Fugman Elementary School
10825 North Cedar Avenue
Fresno, CA 93730-3586
Phone: (559) 327-8700
Principal: Mrs. Tami Graham
School District: Clovis Unified

Jensen Ranch Elementary School
2001 Carson Lane
Castro Valley, CA 94552-1001
Phone: (510) 537-6365
Principal: Mrs. Melodie Stibich
School District: Castro Valley Unified

John Yehall Chin Elementary School
350 Broadway Street
San Francisco, CA 94133-4503
Phone: (415) 291-7946
Principal: Mr. Allen Lee
School District: San Francisco Unified
  School District

Joshua Chadbourne Elementary School
801 Plymouth Avenue
Fremont, CA 94539-4637
Phone: (510) 656-5242
Principal: Ms. Anette Raichbart
School District: Fremont Unified

California (continued)

La Canada Elementary School
4540 Encinas Drive
La Canada, CA 91011-2217
Phone: (818) 952-8350
Principal: Ms. Christine Castillo
School District: La Canada Unified School District

La Reina High School
106 W. Janss Road
Thousand Oaks, CA 91360-3327
Phone: (805) 495-6494
Principal: Dr. Shannon Gomez
School District: Los Angeles Archdiocese

Ocean Air Elementary School
11444 Canter Heights Drive
San Diego, CA 92130-6974
Phone: (858) 481-4040
Principal: Mr. Ryan Stanley
School District: Del Mar Union Elementary

Opal Robinson Elementary School
80 Morningside Drive
Manhattan Beach, CA 90266-6562
Phone: (310) 318-5120
Principal: Ms. Nancy Doyle
School District: Manhattan Beach Unified

Oxford Academy
5172 Orange Avenue
Cypress, CA 90630-2921
Phone: (714) 220-3055
Principal: Mr. Ben Sanchez
School District: Anaheim Union High

Stonegate Elementary School
100 Honors Street
Irvine, CA 92620-2128
Phone: (949) 936-6450
Principal: Mr. Stan Machesky
School District: Irvine Unified School District

Torrey Pines Elementary School
8350 Cliffridge Avenue
La Jolla, CA 92037-2106
Phone: (858) 453-2323
Principal: Ms. Sarah Ott
School District: San Diego Unified

Valley Christian Junior High School
100 Skyway Drive #130
San Jose, CA 95111-3639
Phone: (408) 513-2460
Principal: Mrs. Lisa Arnett
School District: Valley Christian Schools

William Faria Elementary School
10155 Barbara Lane
Cupertino, CA 95014-2901
Phone: (408) 252-0706
Principal: Mrs. Alison Luvara
School District: Cupertino Union

Colorado

Columbia Elementary School
835 E. St. Vrain Street
Colorado Springs, CO 80903-3146
Phone: (719) 328-2700
Principal: Mrs. Karen Shaw
School District: Colorado Springs
   School District 11

Lois Lenski Elementary School
6350 S. Fairfax Way
Littleton, CO 80121-3514
Phone: (303) 347-4575
Principal: Dr. Barbara DeSpain
School District: Littleton 6

Colorado (continued)

Ponderosa Elementary School
1885 S. Lima Street
Aurora, CO 80012-5138
Phone: (720) 747-2800
Principal: Mrs. Elizabeth Sloan
School District: Cherry Creek 5

Ralston Elementary School
25856 Columbine Glen Road
Golden, CO 80401-9616
Phone: (303) 982-4386
Principal: Ms. Dawn Odean
School District: Jefferson County

Traut Core Knowledge School
2515 Timberline Drive
Fort Collins, CO 80528-0000
Phone: (970) 488-7500
Principal: Mr. Mark Wertheimer
School District: Poudre R-1

Connecticut

Bugbee Elementary School
1943 Asylum Avenue
West Hartford, CT 06117-3099
Phone: (860) 233-1234
Principal: Mr. Noam Sturm
School District: West Hartford

St. Jude School
707 Monroe Turnpike
Monroe, CT 06468-2380
Phone: (203) 261-3619
Principal: Mrs. Patricia Griffin
School District: Diocese of Bridgeport

Staples High School
70 North Avenue
Westport, CT 06880-2720
Phone: (203) 341-1210
Principal: Mr. John Dodig
School District: Westport

Weston High School
115 School Road
Weston, CT 06883-1662
Phone: (203) 291-1610
Principal: Mrs. Lisa Wolak Deorio
School District: Weston

Delaware

Allen Frear Elementary School
950 Center Road
Dover, DE 19901-5998
Phone: (302) 697-3279
Principal: Mrs. Tara Faircloth
School District: Caesar Rodney

The Charter School of Wilmington
100 N. DuPont Road
Wilmington, DE 19807-3106
Phone: (302) 651-2727
Principal: Mr. Charles Baldwin

Richard A. Shields Elementary School
910 Shields Avenue
Lewes, DE 19958-5717
Phone: (302) 645-7748
Principal: Mrs. Jennifer Nauman
School District: Cape Henlopen

Department of Defense Education Activity

Kingsolver Elementary School
Bldg 1488, 427 Third Avenue
Fort Knox, DD, Kentucky 40121-7023
Phone: (502) 624-8650
Principal: Ms. Laura Gibson
School District: Kentucky District

Department of Defense Education Activity (continued)

Lakenheath Middle School
DoDDS CCSM Unit 5185 Box 55
APO, DD, Brandon, UK 09461-5555
Phone: (571) 372-6006
Principal: Ms. Mary Zimmerman-Bayer
School District: Isles District

Seoul American Middle School
Unit 15549
APO, DD, Seoul Korea 96205-5549
Phone: (571) 372-0590
Principal: Ms. Maria Dee Buchwald
School District: Korea District

District of Columbia

D.C. Preparatory Academy, Edgewood
  Elementary School Campus
707 Edgewood Street, NE
Washington, DC 20017-3341
Phone: (202) 635-4590
Principal: Ms. Nicole Bryan
School District: D. C. Preparatory Academy

St. Peter School
422 Third Street SE
Washington, DC 20003-1930
Phone: (202) 544-1618
Principal: Mrs. Jennifer Ketchum
School District: Archdiocese of Washington

Florida

Arthur I. Meyer Jewish Academy
3261 N. Military Trail
West Palm Beach, FL 33409-2732
Phone: (561) 686-6520
Principal: Mr. Nehemia Ichilov

Collegiate High School at Northwest
  Florida State College
100 College Boulevard E.
Niceville, FL 32578-1347
Phone: (850) 729-4949
Principal: Mr. Anthony Boyer
School District: Okaloosa County Schools

The First Academy Middle School
2667 Bruton Boulevard
Orlando, FL 32805-5726
Phone: (407) 206-8651
Principal: Dr. Luci Higgins

Hartridge Academy
1400 US Highway 92 West
Winter Haven, FL 33881-8137
Phone: (863) 956-4434
Principal: Ms. Debra Richards
School District: Polk County Public Schools

Georgia

Daves Creek Elementary School
3740 Melody Mizer Lane
Cumming, GA 30041-6940
Phone: (770) 888-1222
Principal: Mr. Eric Ashton
School District: Forsyth County Schools

Fair Oaks Elementary School
407 Barber Road
Marietta, GA 30060-3946
Phone: (678) 594-8080
Principal: Dr. Cindy Szwec
School District: Cobb County School District

Marietta Center for Advanced Academics
311 Aviation Road
Marietta, GA 30060-2463
Phone: (770) 420-0822
Principal: Mrs. Jennifer Hernandez
School District: Marietta City Schools

Georgia (continued)

Middle Ridge Elementary School
11649 South Covington By-Pass Road
Covington, GA 30014-3752
Phone: (770) 385-6463
Principal: Mr. Michael Forehand
School District: Newton County Schools

Mountain Park Elementary School
11895 Mountain Park Road
Roswell, GA 30075-1818
Phone: (770) 552-4530
Principal: Mrs. Stacy Perlman
School District: Fulton County Schools

St. Catherine of Siena Catholic School
1618 Ben King Road
Kennesaw, GA 30144-2945
Phone: (770) 419-8601
Principal: Sister Mary Patrick Connor
School District: Archdiocese of Atlanta

Sugar Hill Elementary School
3259 Athens Highway
Gainesville, GA 30507-8502
Phone: (770) 503-1749
Principal: Ms. Beth Skarda
School District: Hall County Schools

Tritt Elementary School
4435 Post Oak Tritt
Marietta, GA 30062-5622
Phone: (770) 642-5630
Principal: Dr. Karen Frost
School District: Cobb County Schools

Webster County High School
7168 Washington Street
Preston, GA 31824-5232
Phone: (229) 828-3365
Principal: Ms. Janie Downer
School District: Webster County School System

Hawaii

Blanche Pope Elementary School
41-133 Huli Street
Waimanalo, HI 96795-1714
Phone: (808) 259-0450
Principal: Mr. Todd Watanabe
School District: Windward

Nuuanu Elementary School
3055 Puiwa Lane
Honolulu, HI 96817-1126
Phone: (808) 595-5422
Principal: Mr. James Toyooka
School District: Honolulu

Waikiki Elementary School
3710 Leahi Avenue
Honolulu, HI 96815-4429
Phone: (808) 971-6900
Principal: Ms. Bonnie Tabor
School District: Honolulu

Idaho

Gate City Elementary School
2288 Hiskey Street
Pocatello, ID 83201-1815
Phone: (208) 237-2503
Principal: Ms. Deanne Dye
School District: Pocatello/Chubbuck District

Sugar-Salem High School
#1 S. Digger Drive
Sugar City, ID 83448-5014
Phone: (208) 356-0274
Principal: Mr. Jared Jenks
School District: Sugar-Salem Joint District #322

Illinois

Frazier International Magnet School
4027 West Grenshaw Street
Chicago, IL 60624-3930
Phone: (773) 534-6880
Principal: Mr. Faren D'Abell
School District: Chicago Public Schools

Illinois (continued)

Greenbriar Elementary School
1225 Greenbriar Lane
Northbrook, IL 60062-5418
Phone: (847) 498-7950
Principal: Mrs. Jennifer Able
School District: Northbrook School District 28

Lincoln Elementary School
100 S. Nebraska Avenue
Morton, IL 61550-2784
Phone: (309) 266-6989
Principal: Mrs. Sheila Taylor
School District: Morton CUSD 709

Mark T. Skinner West Elementary School
1260 W Adams Street
Chicago, IL 60607-2530
Phone: (773) 534-7790
Principal: Mrs. Deborah Clark
School District: City of Chicago SD 299

Northside Catholic Academy
6216 N. Glenwood Avenue
5525 N. Magnolia Avenue
Chicago, IL 60660-1808
Phone: (773) 743-6277
Principal: Ms. Debra Sullivan
School District: Archdiocese of Chicago

Our Lady of Mount Carmel Academy
720 West Belmont
Chicago, IL 60657-4595
Phone: (773) 525-8779
Principal: Mr. Shane Staszcuk
School District: Archdiocese of Chicago

Prairie Crossing Charter School
1531 Jones Point Road
Grayslake, IL 60030-3536
Phone: (847) 543-9722
Principal: Mrs. Kathleen Lynch
School District: Prairie Crossing Charter School

Queen of Angels School
4520 N. Western Avenue
Chicago, IL 60625-2117
Phone: (773) 769-4211
Principal: Mrs. Julia Byrns Kelly
School District: Archdiocese of Chicago

Roslyn Road Elementary School
224 Roslyn Road
Barrington, IL 60010-2827
Phone: (847) 381-4148
Principal: Mr. Paul Kirk
School District: Barrington Community Unit
    School District 220

St. Joan of Arc School
9245 North Lawndale Avenue
Evanston, IL 60203-0660
Phone: (847) 679-0660
Principal: Mrs. Carrie Hampson
School District: Archdiocese of Chicago

Saint Andrew School
1710 W. Addison Street
Chicago, IL 60613-3580
Phone: (773) 248-2500
Principal: Mr. Allen Ackermann
School District: Archdiocese of Chicago
    Office of Catholic Schools

St. Francis Xavier School
145 N. Waiola Avenue
La Grange, IL 60525-1866
Phone: (708) 352-2175
Principal: Ms. Debra Rodde
School District: Archdiocese of Chicago

St. Michael School
14355 Highland Avenue
Orland Park, IL 60462-2433
Phone: (708) 873-4639
Principal: Mrs. Bernadette Cuttone
School District: Archdiocese of Chicago

Illinois (continued)

Saint Norbert School
1817 Walters Avenue
Northbrook, IL 60062-4595
Phone: (847) 272-0051
Principal: Ms. Rosanne Sikich
School District: Archdiocese of Chicago

St. Peter Lutheran School
111 W. Olive Street
Arlington Heights, IL 60004-4766
Phone: (847) 253-6638
Principal: Mr. Bruce Rudi

Sandburg Middle School
345 E St Charles Road
Elmhurst, IL 60126-3655
Phone: (630) 834-4534
Principal: Ms. Amy Read
School District: Elmhurst SD 205

Scott Elementary School
4732 Patriots Drive
Scott Air Force Base, IL 62225-1197
Phone: (618) 746-4738
Principal: Ms. Cindy Presnell
School District: Mascoutah CUSD 19

The Skokie School
520 Glendale Avenue
Winnetka, IL 60093-2520
Phone: (847) 441-1750
Principal: Ms. April Jordan
School District: Winnetka School District 36

Twin Groves Middle School
2600 N Buffalo Grove Road
Buffalo Grove, IL 60089-8023
Phone: (847) 821-8946
Principal: Mrs. Heather Friziellie
School District: Kildeer Countryside CCSD 96

United North Elementary School
411 W Hunt Avenue
Alexis, IL 61412-8902
Phone: (309) 482-3332
Principal: Mrs. Sue Wilson
School District: United CUSD 304

Wescott Elementary School
1820 Western Avenue
Northbrook, IL 60062-7076
Phone: (847) 272-4660
Principal: Dr. Terri Carman
School District: Northbrook/Glenview SD 30

Indiana

Creekside Middle School
3525 W. 126th Street
Carmel, IN 46032-9557
Phone: (317) 733-6420
Principal: Mr. Thomas Harmas
School District: Carmel Clay Schools

Discovery Middle School
10050 Brummitt Road
Granger, IN 46530-7264
Phone: (574) 674-6010
Principal: Mrs. Sheryll Harper
School District: Penn-Harris-Madison
   School Corporation

Fairmont Elementary School
1725 Abbie Dell Avenue
New Albany, IN 47150-3778
Phone: (812) 542-5501
Principal: Mrs. Susan Gahan
School District: New Albany Floyd County
Consolidated School Corporation

Indiana (continued)

Holy Family School
990 E. Church Avenue
Jasper, IN 47546-3715
Phone: (812) 482-4485
Principal: Mrs. Sally Sternberg
School District: Diocese of Evansville

Jonas E. Salk Elementary School
3001 W 77th Avenue
Merrillville, IN 46410-3586
Phone: (219) 650-5304
Principal: Mrs. Kara Bonin
School District: Merrillville School Corporation

Laura G. Childs Elementary School
2211 S High Street
Bloomington, IN 47401-4315
Phone: (812) 330-7756
Principal: Mr. Chris Finley
School District: Monroe County
   Community School Corporation

Morgan Township Elementary School
299 South State Road 49
Valparaiso, IN 46383-7976
Phone: (219) 462-5883
Principal: Mrs. Michelle Friesen-Carper
School District: East Porter County
   School Corporation

New Haven Intermediate School
1065 Woodmere Drive
New Haven, IN 46774-2300
Phone: (260) 446-0190
Principal: Mrs. Alicia Gatewood
School District: East Allen County Schools

Pine Ridge Elementary School
4613 S. Pine Ridge Road
Birdseye, IN 47513-9745
Phone: (812) 326-2324
Principal: Mr. Ryan Haas
School District: Southeast Dubois
   Consolidated School Corporation

Saint Louis de Montfort Catholic School
11421 Hague Road
Fishers, IN 46038-1876
Phone: (317) 842-1125
Principal: Mrs. Annette Marie Jones
School District: Diocese of Lafayette

Saint Maria Goretti School
17104 Spring Mill Road
Westfield, IN 46074-9673
Phone: (317) 503-5674
Principal: Mr. Vince Barnes
School District: Diocese of Lafayette-in-Indiana

Trinity School at Greenlawn
107 South Greenlawn Avenue
South Bend, IN 46617-3430
Phone: (574) 287-5590
Principal: Mr. John Lee

Iowa

Harlan Community High School
2102 Durant Street
Harlan, IA 51537-1221
Phone: (712) 755-3101
Principal: Mr. John Connell
School District: Harlan Community School District

Herbert Hoover Elementary School
3223 S. Hampton Drive
Bettendorf, IA 52722-2685
Phone: (563) 359-8263
Principal: Mr. Jeffrey Johannsen
School District: Bettendorf Community
   School District

Meeker Elementary School
300 20th Street
Ames, IA 50010-4906
Phone: (515) 239-3770
Principal: Mr. Steve Flynn
School District: Ames Community School District

Iowa (continued)

Okoboji Elementary School
705 N. Avenue
Milford, IA 51351-0147
Phone: (712) 338-2458
Principal: Mr. Justin Bouse
School District: Okoboji Community
  School District

Taft Elementary School
612 2nd Avenue North
Humboldt, IA 50548-8867
Phone: (515) 332-3216
Principal: Mr. George Bruder
School District: Humboldt Community
  School District

Kansas

Campus High School
2100 W. 55th Street South
Wichita, KS 67217-4199
Phone: (316) 554-2236
Principal: Mr. Myron Regier
School District: Haysville USD 261

Chapman High School
400 W. 4th Street
Box 249
Chapman, KS 67431-0249
Phone: (785) 922-6561
Principal: Mr. Kevin Suther
School District: Chapman

Mission Trail Elementary School
13200 Mission Road
Leawood, KS 66209-1750
Phone: (913) 239-6700
Principal: Ms. Debra Bond
School District: Blue Valley

Oswego Neosho Heights Elementary School
12 Oregon Street
Box 129
Oswego, KS 67356-0129
Phone: (620) 795-4541
Principal: Mrs. Janie Allison
School District: Oswego

West Franklin High School
511 East Franklin Street
Pomona, KS 66076-9768
Phone: (785) 566-3392
Principal: Mr. Rick Smith
School District: West Franklin

Kentucky

Auburn Elementary School
221 College Street
Auburn, KY 42206-5310
Phone: (270) 542-4181
Principal: Mr. David Ward
School District: Logan County Schools

Beechwood High School
54 Beechwood Road
Ft. Mitchell, KY 41017-2716
Phone: (859) 331-1220
Principal: Mr. Ben Zimmerman
School District: Beechwood Independent
  School District

Glendover Elementary School
710 Glendover Road
Lexington, KY 40502-2846
Phone: (859) 381-3403
Principal: Dr. Catherine Fine
School District: Fayette County Public Schools

Mann Elementary School
10435 U.S. Highway 42
Union, KY 41091-9528
Phone: (859) 384-5000
Principal: Ms. Connie Crigger
School District: Boone County School District

Kentucky (continued)

Star Elementary School
8249 E. U.S. Highway 60
P.O. Box 485
Rush, KY 41168-8804
Phone: (606) 474-5756
Principal: Mr. Charles Baker
School District: Carter County School District

Louisiana

Ella Dolhonde Elementary School
219 Severn Avenue
Metairie, LA 70001-5198
Phone: (504) 837-5370
Principal: Mrs. Mathilde J. Wimberly
School District: Jefferson Parish Public Schools

Haynes Academy School for Advanced Studies
1416 Metairie Road
Metairie, LA 70005-3921
Phone: (504) 837-8300
Principal: Ms. Karla Russo
School District: Jefferson Parish
  Public School System

Lake Forest Elementary Charter School
12000 Hayne Boulevard
New Orleans, LA 70128-1127
Phone: (504) 826-7140
Principal: Ms. Mardele S. Early
School District: Orleans Parish School Board

Morehouse Magnet School
909 Larche Lane
Bastrop, LA 71220-2924
Phone: (318) 281-3126
Principal: Ms. Gwendolyn Seay
School District: Morehouse Public School Board

Most Blessed Sacrament School
8033 Baringer Road
Baton Rouge, LA 70817-6012
Phone: (225) 751-0273
Principal: Mrs. Maria Cloessner
School District: Diocese of Baton Rouge

Pearl Watson Elementary School
1300 Fifth Street
Lake Charles, LA 70601-6308
Phone: (337) 217-4860
Principal: Mr. Rodney Geyen
School District: Calcasieu Parish

Maine

Williams-Cone School
19 Perkins Street
Topsham, ME 04086-1804
Phone: (207) 725-4391
Principal: Mrs. Randa Rineer
School District: RSU 75

Maryland

Boonsboro High School
10 Campus Avenue
Boonsboro, MD 21713-1108
Phone: (301) 766-8022
Principal: Mrs. Peggy Pugh
School District: Washington County
  Public Schools

Century High School
355 Ronsdale Road
Sykesville, MD 21784-8956
Phone: (410) 386-4400
Principal: Mr. Randy Clark
School District: Carroll County Public Schools

Chadwick Elementary School
1918 Winder Road
Baltimore, MD 21244-1729
Phone: (410) 887-1300
Principal: Mrs. Bonnie Hess
School District: Baltimore County Public Schools

Maryland (continued)

Charlesmont Elementary School
7800 West Collingham Drive
Baltimore, MD 21222-2598
Phone: (410) 887-7004
Principal: Ms. Marsha Ayres
School District: Baltimore County Public Schools

Folly Quarter Middle School
13500 Tridelphia Road
Ellicott City, MD 21042-1134
Phone: (410) 313-1506
Principal: Mr. Rick Wilson
School District: Howard County
   Public School System

Holy Cross Catholic School
4900 Strathmore Avenue
PO Box 249
Garrett Park, MD 20896-0249
Phone: (301) 949-0053
Principal: Mrs. Lisa Maio Kane
School District: Archdiocese of Washington

Robert Frost Middle School
9201 Scott Drive
Rockville, MD 20850-3441
Phone: (301) 279-3949
Principal: Dr. Joey Jones
School District: Montgomery County
   Public School

St. John the Evangelist School
10201 Woodland Drive
Silver Spring, MD 20902-3851
Phone: (301) 681-7656
Principal: Sister Kathleen Lannak
School District: Archdiocese of Washington

St. Joseph School - Cockeysville
105 Church Lane
Cockeysville, MD 21030-4998
Phone: (410) 683-0600
Principal: Mr. Terrance Golden
School District: Archdiocese of Baltimore

Saint Margaret School
205 Hickory Avenue
Bel Air, MD 21014-3241
Phone: (410) 877-9660
Principal: Mrs. Madeleine Hobik
School District: Archdiocese of Baltimore

St. Mary's Elementary School
111 Duke of Gloucester Street
Annapolis, MD 21401-2599
Phone: (410) 263-2869
Principal: Mrs. Rebecca Zimmerman
School District: Archdiocese of Baltimore

Massachusetts

Jonas Clarke Middle School
17 Stedman Road
Lexington, MA 02421-7125
Phone: (781) 861-2450
Principal: Mrs. Anna Monaco
School District: Lexington Public Schools

New Mission High School
655 Metropolitan Avenue
Hyde Park, MA 02136-3650
Phone: (617) 635-6437
Principal: Mrs. Naia Wilson
School District: Boston Public Schools

Winchester High School
80 Skillings Road
Winchester, MA 01890-2853
Phone: (781) 721-7020
Principal: Dr. Thomas Gwin
School District: Winchester Public Schools

Worcester Technical High School
1 Skyline Drive
Worcester, MA 01605-2885
Phone: (508) 799-1940
Principal: Ms. Sheila Harrity
School District: Worcester Public Schools

Minnesota

Bendix Elementary School
655 Park Street East
Annandale, MN 55302-0190
Phone: (320) 274-8218
Principal: Mrs. Allyson Kuehn
School District: Annandale Public Schools

Deephaven Elementary School
4452 Vine Hill Road
Deephaven, MN 55391-3539
Phone: (952) 401-6900
Principal: Mr. Bryan McGinley
School District: Minnetonka Public Schools

Delano Elementary School
678 Tiger Drive
Delano, MN 55328-8727
Phone: (763) 972-3365
Principal: Mr. Darren Schuler
School District: Delano Public School District

Garfield Elementary School
303 Sanstead Street East
Box 158
Garfield, MN 56332-0158
Phone: (320) 834-2261
Principal: Ms. Lisa Pikop
School District: Alexandria Public School District

Hanover Elementary School
274 Labeaux Avenue NE
Hanover, MN 55341-4003
Phone: (763) 682-0823
Principal: Mr. Jeff Olson
School District: Buffalo-Hanover-Montrose Public

International Spanish Language Academy
5959 Shady Oak Road
Minnetonka, MN 55343-8969
Phone: (952) 746-6020
Principal: Ms. Karen Terhaar
School District: International Spanish
   Language Academy

Winsted Elementary School
431 4th Street North
Winsted, MN 55395-0160
Phone: (320) 485-2190
Principal: Mrs. Jennifer Olson
School District: Howard Lake-Waverly-Winsted

Mississippi

DeLisle Elementary School
6303 W Wittman Road
Pass Christian, MS 39571-8518
Phone: (228) 255-6219
Principal: Ms. Desiree Lizana
School District: Pass Christian School District

East Hancock Elementary School
4221 Kiln Delisle Road
Kiln, MS 39556-6695
Phone: (228) 255-6637
Principal: Ms. Tara Ladner
School District: Hancock County School District

Lovett Elementary School
2002 West Northside Drive
Clinton, MS 39056-3014
Phone: (601) 924-5664
Principal: Mr. Mike Pope
School District: Clinton Public

Oak Park Elementary School
2230 Government Street
Ocean Springs, MS 39566-7002
Phone: (228) 875-5847
Principal: Dr. Jennifer Pope
School District: Ocean Springs

Missouri

Bolivar High School
1401 N Highway D
Bolivar, MO 65613-8282
Phone: (417) 326-5228
Principal: Dr. David Geurin
School District: Bolivar R-I

Missouri (continued)

Brentwood High School
2221 High School Drive
Brentwood, MO 63144-1725
Phone: (314) 962-3837
Principal: Dr. Edward Johnson
School District: Brentwood School District

Lee's Summit West High School
2600 Southwest Ward Road
Lee's Summit, MO 64082-2107
Phone: (816) 986-4000
Principal: Dr. David Sharp
School District: Lee's Summit R-7 School District

Messiah Lutheran School
5911 S. Highway 94
St. Charles, MO 63304-5611
Phone: (636) 329-1096
Principal: Dr. Tom Guenzler

Nixa High School
301 S. Main Street
Nixa, MO 65714-8663
Phone: (417) 724-3500
Principal: Mr. Mark McGehee
School District: Nixa Public Schools

Sappington Elementary School
11011 Gravois Road
St. Louis, MO 63126-5860
Phone: (314) 729-2460
Principal: Mr. Craig Hamby
School District: Lindbergh Schools

Spokane High School
1123 Spokane Road
PO Box 218
Spokane, MO 65754-0218
Phone: (417) 443-3502
Principal: Mr. Mike Morelock
School District: Spokane R-VII

W.W. Keysor School
725 North Geyer Road
Kirkwood, MO 63122-2701
Phone: (314) 213-6120
Principal: Dr. Bryan Painter
School District: Kirkwood R-VII

Willow Springs High School
215 W. Fourth Street
Willow Springs, MO 65793-1118
Phone: (417) 469-2114
Principal: Mrs. Jimalee James
School District: Willow Springs R-IV

Montana

Manhattan Elementary School
416 North Broadway
P.O. Box 425
Manhattan, MT 59741-0425
Phone: (406) 284-3250
Principal: Mr. Scott Schumacher
School District: Manhattan School

Nebraska

Burwell Elementary School
204 S. 4th Street
PO Box 790
Burwell, NE 68823-0790
Phone: (308) 346-4431
Principal: Mr. Gordon Goodman
School District: Burwell Public Schools

Ord Elementary School
820 S 16th Street
Ord, NE 68862-1984
Phone: (308) 728-3331
Principal: Mr. Doug Smith
School District: Ord Public Schools

Nebraska (continued)

St. Patrick's Catholic School-Elkhorn
20500 West Maple Road
PO Box 10
Elkhorn, NE 68022-0010
Phone: (402) 289-5407
Principal: Mr. Don Ridder
School District: Archdiocese of Omaha

Wakefield Elementary School
802 Highland Street
PO Box 330
Wakefield, NE 68784-0330
Phone: (402) 287-9892
Principal: Mr. Jerad Wulf
School District: Wakefield Community Schools

Wisner-Pilger Elementary School
801 18th Street
PO Box 580
Wisner, NE 68791-0580
Phone: (402) 529-6465
Principal: Mr. Mark Porter
School District: Wisner-Pilger Public Schools

Nevada

Elizabeth Lenz Elementary School
2500 Homeland Drive
Reno, NV 89511-9239
Phone: (775) 851-5620
Principal: Mrs. Teri Vaughan
School District: Washoe County School District

Ted Hunsberger School
2505 Crossbow Court
Reno, NV 89511-5301
Phone: (775) 851-7095
Principal: Ms. Jenny Ricci
School District: Washoe County School District

Walter Bracken STEAM Academy
1200 North 27th Street
Las Vegas, NV 89101-1517
Phone: (702) 799-7095
Principal: Ms. Kathleen Decker
School District: Clark County School District

New Hampshire

Hollis Primary School
36 Silver Lake Road
Hollis, NH 03049-6286
Phone: (603) 324-5995
Principal: Mrs. Elizabeth Allen
School District: Hollis School District

Lin-Wood Public Elementary School
72 Linwood Drive
Lincoln, NH 03251-0097
Phone: (603) 745-2214
Principal: Ms. Gale Adams
School District: Lincoln-Woodstock Cooperative

Newfields Elementary School
9 Piscassic Road
Newfields, NH 03856-8206
Phone: (603) 772-5555
Principal: Mrs. Helen Rist
School District: SAU 16-Newfields

New Jersey

Academy for Information Technology
1776 Raritan Road
Scotch Plains, NJ 07076-2928
Phone: (908) 889-8288
Principal: Mrs. Gloria Griffith
School District: Union County Vocational
   Technical School District

New Jersey (continued)

Academy of Our Lady
180 Rodney Street
Glen Rock, NJ 07452-2826
Phone: (201) 445-0622
Principal: Mrs. Patricia Keenaghan
School District: Archdiocese of Newark

Aquinas Academy
388 South Livingston Avenue
Livingston, NJ 07039-3914
Phone: (973) 992-1587
Principal: Sister Lena Picillo
School District: Archdiocese of Newark

Dover High School
100 Grace Street
Dover, NJ 07801-2644
Phone: (973) 989-2010
Principal: Mr. Delvis Rodriguez
School District: Dover Public School District

Harrison High School
800 Hamilton Street
Harrison, NJ 07029-1405
Phone: (973) 482-5050
Principal: Mr. Ronald F. Shields
School District: Harrison Public Schools

High Tech High School
2000 85th Street
North Bergen, NJ 07047-4715
Phone: (201) 662-6801
Principal: Dr. Joseph Giammarella
School District: Hudson County
  Schools of Technology

Immaculate Conception School
314 Old Allerton Road
Annandale, NJ 08801-3215
Phone: (908) 735-6334
Principal: Mrs. Annamarie Reilly
School District: Diocese of Metuchen

Marine Academy of Science and Technology
305 Mast Way
Sandy Hook, NJ 07732-4004
Phone: (732) 291-0995
Principal: Dr. Paul J. Christopher
School District: Monmouth County
  Vocational School District

Middlesex County Academy for Science,
  Mathematics & Engineering Technologies
100 Technology Drive
Edison, NJ 08837-3644
Phone: (732) 452-2600
Principal: Dr. Linda Russo
School District: Middlesex County
  Vocational and Technical Schools

Morris County School of Technology
400 East Main Street
Denville, NJ 07834-2516
Phone: (973) 627-4600
Principal: Mr. Scott Moffitt
School District: Morris County
  Vocational School District

Rabbi Pesach Raymon Yeshiva
2 Harrison Street
Edison, NJ 08817-2907
Phone: (732) 572-5052
Principal: Rabbi Shraga Gross

St. Francis Academy
1601 Central Avenue
Union City, NJ 07087-3216
Phone: (201) 863-4112
Principal: Ms. Deborah Savage
School District: Archdiocese of Newark

St. Rose of Lima Academy
52 Short Hills Avenue
Short Hills, NJ 07078-2529
Phone: (973) 379-3973
Principal: Mrs. Diane Pollak
School District: Archdiocese of Newark

New Jersey (continued)

Union County Magnet High School
1776 Raritan Road
Scotch Plains, NJ 07076-2997
Phone: (908) 889-8288
Principal: Mrs. Gwendolyn Ryan
School District: Union County Vocational
   Technical School District

Wildwood High School
4300 Pacific Avenue
Wildwood, NJ 08260-4625
Phone: (609) 522-7922
Principal: Mr. Christopher Armstrong
School District: Wildwood City
   Board of Education

New Mexico

Albuquerque Institute of Math & Science
   at UNM Charter School
933 Bradbury SE
Albuquerque, NM 87106-4374
Phone: (505) 559-4249
Principal: Ms. Kathy Sandoval
School District: State of New Mexico
   Chartered School

Anthony Elementary School
600 N. Fourth Street
Anthony, NM 88021-0000
Phone: (575) 882-4561
Principal: Ms. Linda L. Perez
School District: Gadsden Independent Schools

Holloman Middle School
381 1st Street Building. 768, Holloman AFB
PO Box 650
Alamogordo, NM 88311-0650
Phone: (575) 812-6200
Principal: Ms. Maria Showalter
School District: Alamogordo Public School

New York

Bayville Elementary School
50 Mountain Avenue
Bayville, NY 11709-2002
Phone: (516) 277-5400
Principal: Mr. Scott McElhiney
School District: Locust Valley CSD

Cherry Lane Elementary School
1 Heather Drive
Suffern, NY 10901-6613
Phone: (845) 357-3988
Principal: Dr. David Leach
School District: Ramapo CSD

Cherry Road Elementary School
201 Cherry Road
Syracuse, NY 13219-1598
Phone: (315) 426-3300
Principal: Mrs. Sarah Vanliew
School District: Westhill CSD

Elsmere Elementary School
247 Delaware Avenue
Delmar, NY 12054-1499
Phone: (518) 439-4996
Principal: Mrs. Katherine Kloss
School District: Bethlehem Central School District

Harrison Avenue Elementary School
480 Harrison Avenue
Harrison, NY 10528-2118
Phone: (914) 630-3192
Principal: Ms. Valerie Hymes
School District: Harrison CSD

Kramer Lane Elementary School
1 Kramer Lane
Plainview, NY 11803-6013
Phone: (516) 644-4501
Principal: Ms. Kerri McCarthy
School District: Bethpage UFSD

New York (continued)

Leo Bernabi School
1 Bernabi Road
Spencerport, NY 14559-1899
Phone: (585) 349-5402
Principal: Ms. Andrea Campo
School District: Spencerport CSD

Maple West Elementary School
851 Maple Road
Williamsville, NY 14221-3260
Phone: (716) 626-8840
Principal: Dr. Charles Galluzzo
School District: Williamsville Central
   School District

PS 46 Queens The Alley Pond School
64-45 218th Street
Oakland Gardens, NY 11364-2237
Phone: (718) 423-8395
Principal: Mrs. Marsha Goldberg
School District: NYC District 26

PS 066 Queens Jacqueline Kennedy
   Onassis School
85-11 102nd Street
Richmond Hill, NY 11418-1147
Phone: (718) 849-0184
Principal: Mrs. Phyllis Leinwand
School District: NYC District 27

PS 199 Jessie Isador Straus School
270 W. 70th Street
New York, NY 10023-5006
Phone: (212) 799-1033
Principal: Ms. Katy Rosen
School District: NYC District 3

PS 221 The North Hills School
57-40 Marathon Parkway
Little Neck, NY 11362-2036
Phone: (718) 423-8825
Principal: Mrs. Patricia Bullard
School District: NYC District 26

PS 222 Katherine R. Snyder School
3301 Quentin Road
Brooklyn, NY 11234-4241
Phone: (718) 998-4298
Principal: Mrs. Theresa Olivieri
School District: NYC District 22

PS 247 School
7000 21st Avenue
Brooklyn, NY 11204-5404
Phone: (718) 236-4205
Principal: Mr. Christopher Ogno
School District: NYC District 20

Shaw Avenue School
99 Shaw Avenue
Valley Stream, NY 11580-3195
Phone: (516) 872-4320
Principal: Ms. Johane Ligonde
School District: Valley Stream 30 UFSD

South Davis Elementary School
51 S. Davis Street
Orchard Park, NY 14127-2605
Phone: (716) 209-6246
Principal: Mrs. Christine Rassow
School District: Orchard Park CSD

Tesago Elementary School
970 Route 146
Clifton Park, NY 12065-3684
Phone: (518) 881-0570
Principal: Mr. Gregory Pace
School District: Shenendehowa CSD

West Side School
1597 Laurel Hollow Road
Syosset, NY 11791-9636
Phone: (516) 692-7900
Principal: Mr. Kurt Simon
School District: Cold Spring Harbor CSD

North Carolina

Greene Early College High School
818 Highway 91
Snow Hill, NC 28580-7286
Phone: (252) 747-9044
Principal: Mr. Charlie Langley
School District: Greene County Schools

Middle College of NC A & T
1601 East Market Street
Greensboro, NC 27411-0002
Phone: (336) 691-0941
Principal: Mr. Eric Hines
School District: Guilford County Schools

Providence Spring Elementary School
10045 Providence Church Lane
Charlotte, NC 28277-9723
Phone: (980) 343-6935
Principal: Ms. Diane Adams
School District: Charlotte-Mecklenburg Schools

Rutherford Early College High
286 ICC Loop Road
Spindale, NC 28160-0804
Phone: (828) 395-4190
Principal: Mr. Jeremiah McCluney
School District: Rutherford County Schools

Shiloh Elementary School
5210 Rogers Road
Monroe, NC 28110-8527
Phone: (704) 296-3035
Principal: Mr. Scott Spencer
School District: Union County Public Schools

Weddington Middle School
5903 Deal Road
Matthews, NC 28104-7973
Phone: (704) 814-9772
Principal: Mr. Steven Wray
School District: Union County Public Schools

North Dakota

Edgeley Public School
PO Box 37
Edgeley, ND 58433-0037
Phone: (701) 493-2292
Principal: Mr. Garitt Irey
School District: Edgeley 3

William S. Gussner Elementary School
PO Box 269
Jamestown, ND 58401-0269
Phone: (701) 252-3846
Principal: Mrs. Peg Wagner
School District: Jamestown 1

Wyndmere Elementary School
101 Date Avenue
PO Box 190
Wyndmere, ND 58081-0190
Phone: (701) 439-2287
Principal: Mr. David Hanson
School District: Wyndmere Public
   School District #42

Ohio

Akron Early College High School
225 S. Main Street
Akron, OH 44325-6001
Phone: (330) 972-6450
Principal: Ms. Marilyn Bennett
School District: Akron Public Schools

Cuyahoga Heights High School
4820 East 71st
Cuyahoga Heights, OH 44125-1095
Phone: (216) 429-5700
Principal: Mr. Thomas Evans
School District: Cuyahoga Heights
   Local School District

Ohio (continued)

Harmon Middle School
130 Aurora-Hudson Road
Aurora, OH 44202-9234
Phone: (330) 954-2101
Principal: Mr. Mark Abramovich
School District: Aurora City School District

Incarnate Word Academy
6620 Pearl Road
Parma Heights, OH 44130-3808
Phone: (440) 842-6818
Principal: Mrs. Janette Cicerchi
School District: Diocese of Cleveland

Incarnation Catholic School
45 Williamsburg Lane
Centerville, OH 45459-4218
Phone: (937) 433-1051
Principal: Dr. Cheryl Reichel
School District: Archdiocese of Cincinnati

Newton Elementary School
201 N. Long Street
Pleasant Hill, OH 45359-8077
Phone: (937) 676-2002
Principal: Ms. Danielle Davis
School District: Newton Local School District

Orchard Middle School
6800 S.O.M. Center Road
Solon, OH 44139-4133
Phone: (440) 349-6218
Principal: Mrs. Cari Mineard
School District: Solon City School District

St. Margaret of York School
9495 Columbia Road
Loveland, OH 45140-1560
Phone: (513) 683-9793
Principal: Mr. Kevin Vance
School District: Archdiocese of Cincinnati

St. Paul The Apostle Catholic School
61 Moss Road
Westerville, OH 43082-9054
Phone: (614) 882-2710
Principal: Dr. Kathleen Norris
School District: Diocese of Columbus

Scioto Elementary School
20 W. Scioto Street
Commercial Point, OH 43116-9712
Phone: (740) 983-3221
Principal: Mr. Robin Halley
School District: Teays Valley Local

Springfield Elementary School
10580 Main Street
New Middletown, OH 44442-9701
Phone: (330) 542-2929
Principal: Mr. Thomas Yazvac
School District: Springfield Local School District

Waterville Primary School
457 Sycamore Lane
Waterville, OH 43566-1253
Phone: (419) 878-2436
Principal: Dr. Chad Warnimont
School District: Anthony Wayne Local

Watson Elementary School
515 Marion Avenue
Massillon, OH 44646-3005
Phone: (330) 832-8100
Principal: Mr. Nicholas Huskins
School District: Perry Local School District

West Geauga High School
13401 Chillicothe Road
Chesterland, OH 44026-3532
Phone: (440) 729-5955
Principal: Mr. Jay Bishop
School District: West Geauga Local

Ohio (continued)

Wheelersburg Elementary School
800 Pirate Drive
Wheelersburg, OH 45694-9088
Phone: (740) 574-8130
Principal: Mrs. Janeen Spradlin
School District: Wheelersburg
  Local School District

Oklahoma

Bartlesville Mid-High School
5900 Baylor Drive
Bartlesville, OK 74006-8909
Phone: (918) 333-4444
Principal: Mr. Jason Langham
School District: Bartlesville Public Schools

Central High Elementary School
7202 West Broncho Road
Marlow, OK 73055-9599
Phone: (580) 658-2970
Principal: Mrs. LeAnn Johnson
School District: Central High Public Schools

Chisholm High School
4018 West Carrier Road
Enid, OK 73703-1018
Phone: (580) 233-2852
Principal: Ms. Jaymie Morley
School District: Chisholm Public Schools

Harding Charter Preparatory High School
3333 North Shartel Avenue
Oklahoma City, OK 73118-7277
Phone: (405) 528-0562
Principal: Mr. Justin Hunt

Tulsa Eisenhower International
  Elementary School
2819 South New Haven Avenue
Tulsa, OK 74114-5937
Phone: (918) 746-9100
Principal: Ms. Belinda Baldwin
School District: Tulsa Public Schools

Wayland Bonds Elementary School
14025 South May Avenue
Oklahoma City, OK 73170-2014
Phone: (405) 735-4500
Principal: Ms. Michelle McNear
School District: Moore Public Schools

Pennsylvania

Bart-Colerain Elementary School
1336 Noble Road
Christiana, PA 17509-9768
Phone: (717) 529-2181
Principal: Mrs. Sandra Haines
School District: Solanco School District

Fort Couch Middle School
515 Fort Couch Road
Upper St. Clair, PA 15241-2099
Phone: (412) 833-1600
Principal: Mr. Joseph DeMar
School District: Upper St. Clair School District

The Laboratory Charter School of
  Communication and Languages
124 Bryn Mawr Avenue
Bala Cynwyd, PA 19004-0000
Phone: (610) 617-9121
Principal: Mrs. LaKeisha Patrick
School District: Charter

Laurel Point Elementary School
1141 Airport Road
Vandergrift, PA 15690-6017
Phone: (724) 568-2552
Principal: Mr. Jeffrey Jackson
School District: Kiski School District

Lincoln Elementary School
2 Ralston Place
Pittsburgh, PA 15216-1524
Phone: (412) 344-2147
Principal: Dr. Marybeth Irvin
School District: Mount Lebanon

Pennsylvania (continued)

Loganville-Springfield Elementary School
169 North Main Street
York, PA 17403-9808
Phone: (717) 428-2240
Principal: Mr. Scott Carl
School District: Dallastown Area School District

Northwest Pennsylvania Collegiate
  Academy High School
2825 State Street
Erie, PA 16508-1563
Phone: (814) 874-6301
Principal: Dr. Tammie Smith
School District: Erie City School District

Peters Township Middle School
625 East McMurray Road
McMurray, PA 15317-3497
Phone: (724) 941-2688
Principal: Dr. Robert Freado
School District: Peters Township School District

Saint Andrew School
51 Wrights Road
Newtown, PA 18940-1334
Phone: (215) 968-2685
Principal: Mrs. Nancy Matteo
School District: Archdiocese of Philadelphia

Saint Patrick School
115 Channing Ave
Malvern, PA 19355-2747
Phone: (610) 644-5797
Principal: Ms. Patricia O'Donnell
School District: Archdiocese of Philadelphia

Souderton Collaborative Charter School
110 E. Broad Street
Souderton, PA 18964-1276
Phone: (215) 721-4560
Principal: Ms. Jennifer Arevalo
School District: Souderton Charter
  School Collaborative

Southmoreland Elementary School
100 Scottie Way
Scottdale, PA 15683-1048
Phone: (724) 887-2021
Principal: Mr. John Lee
School District: Southmoreland

Tidioute Community Charter School
241 Main Street
Tidioute, PA 16351-1222
Phone: (814) 484-3550
Principal: Mr. Douglas Allen
School District: Charter

Whitemarsh Elementary School
4120 Joshua Road
Lafayette Hill, PA 19444-1213
Phone: (610) 828-9092
Principal: Mrs. Donna Drizin
School District: Colonial

Wycallis Elementary School
2010 Conyngham Avenue
Dallas, PA 18612-0720
Phone: (570) 674-7283
Principal: Dr. Paul Reinert
School District: Dallas School District

Rhode Island

Stony Lane Elementary School
825 Stony Lane
North Kingstown, RI 02852-3699
Phone: (401) 268-6540
Principal: Mr. Edward Ferrario
School District: North Kingstown
  School Department

Rhode Island (continued)

William M. Davies, Jr. Career and
   Technical High School
50 Jenckes Hill Road
Lincoln, RI 02865-4602
Phone: (401) 728-1500
Principal: Ms. Victoria Gailliard-Garrick
School District: Davies, Jr. Career and Technical

South Carolina

Flowertown Elementary School
20 King Charles Circle
Summerville, SC 29485-3402
Phone: (843) 871-7400
Principal: Ms. Donna Goodwin
School District: Dorchester School District 2

Mayo High School for Math,
   Science & Technology
405 Chestnut Street
Darlington, SC 29532-5211
Phone: (843) 398-2650
Principal: Mrs. Arlene Wallace
School District: Darlington County School District

New Prospect Elementary School
9251 Highway 9
Inman, SC 29349-6982
Phone: (864) 592-1970
Principal: Mrs. Jodi Wright
School District: Spartanburg School District 1

Okatie Elementary School
53 Cherry Point Road
Okatie, SC 29909-3759
Phone: (843) 322-7700
Principal: Mrs. Jamie Pinckney
School District: Beaufort County School District

Ware Shoals Elementary School
45 West Main Street
Ware Shoals, SC 29692-1499
Phone: (864) 456-2711
Principal: Ms. Nancy Brown
School District: Ware Shoals School District 51

South Dakota

Faulkton Elementary School
PO Box 308
1114 Court Street
Faulkton, SD 57438-0308
Phone: (605) 598-6266
Principal: Dr. Joel Price
School District: Faulkton Area Schools

Gertie Belle Rogers Elementary School
1301 N Kimball Avenue
Mitchell, SD 57301-7760
Phone: (605) 995-3091
Principal: Mrs. Vicki Harmdierks
School District: Mitchell School District

Harvey Dunn Elementary School
2400 S. Bahnson Avenue
Sioux Falls, SD 57103-4462
Phone: (605) 371-4120
Principal: Mrs. Teresa Boysen
School District: Sioux Falls School District

St. Joseph School
210 E. Broadway
Pierre, SD 57501-2299
Phone: (605) 224-7185
Principal: Mrs. Darlene Braun
School District: Saints Peter &
   Paul Parish School

Tennessee

Holy Rosary Academy
190 Graylynn Drive
Nashville, TN 37214-2706
Phone: (615) 883-1108
Principal: Dr. Betty Reynolds
School District: Diocese of Nashville

McFadden School of Excellence
221 Bridge Avenue
Murfreesboro, TN 37129-3503
Phone: (615) 893-7251
Principal: Dr. Clark Blair
School District: Rutherford County Schools

Tennessee (continued)

Meigs Middle Magnet School
713 Ramsey Street
Nashville, TN 37206-4015
Phone: (615) 271-3222
Principal: Dr. Samuel Underwood
School District: Metropolitan Nashville
  Public Schools

Thomas Magnet School
515 Tate Avenue
Shelbyville, TN 37160-3288
Phone: (931) 684-6818
Principal: Ms. Janice Womble
School District: Bedford County Schools

Utah

Central Elementary School
95 North 400 East
Pleasant Grove, UT 84062-2899
Phone: (801) 785-8711
Principal: Dr. Vicki Carter
School District: Alpine District

Virginia

Carrsville Elementary School
5355 Carrsville Highway
Carrsville, VA 23315-3024
Phone: (757) 357-8844
Principal: Ms. Laura Matthews
School District: Isle of Wight County
  Public Schools

Forest Hills Elementary School
155 Mount View Avenue
Danville, VA 24541-0000
Phone: (434) 799-6430
Principal: Ms. Catherine Lassiter
School District: Danville Public Schools

Garrisonville Elementary School
100 Wood Drive
Stafford, VA 22556-1838
Phone: (540) 658-6260
Principal: Ms. Alexis White
School District: Stafford County Public Schools

L. L. Beazley Elementary School
6700 Courthouse Road
Prince George, VA 23875-2533
Phone: (804) 733-2745
Principal: Mr. James Scruggs
School District: Prince George County
  Public Schools

Meriwether Lewis Elementary School
1610 Owensville Road
Charlottesville, VA 22901-9407
Phone: (434) 293-9304
Principal: Ms. Kimberly Cousins
School District: Albemarle County Public Schools

Sacred Heart Academy
110 Keating Drive
Winchester, VA 22601-2899
Phone: (540) 662-7177
Principal: Mrs. Rebecca McTavish
School District: Diocese of Arlington

St. Veronica Catholic School
3460B Centreville Road
Chantilly, VA 20151-3038
Phone: (703) 773-2023
Principal: Mr. Peter Mannix
School District: Arlington Diocese

Saint Patrick Catholic School
1000 Bolling Avenue
Norfolk, VA 23508-1604
Phone: (757) 440-5500
Principal: Mr. Stephen Hammond

Virginia (continued)

Snowville Elementary School
4858 Lead Mine Road
Hiwassee, VA 24347-2814
Phone: (540) 643-0766
Principal: Dr. Bridget Parsons
School District: Pulaski County Public Schools

Westbriar Elementary School
1741 Pine Valley Drive
Vienna, VA 22182-2340
Phone: (703) 937-1700
Principal: Mrs. Lisa Pilson
School District: Fairfax County Public Schools

West Virginia

Monongah Middle School
550 Camden Avenue
Monongah, WV 26554-1105
Phone: (304) 367-2164
Principal: Mr. C. Steven Malnick
School District: Marion County
   Board of Education

Panther Creek Elementary School
10068 Canvas Nettie Road
Nettie, WV 26681-0339
Phone: (304) 846-6808
Principal: Ms. Angela Amick
School District: Nicholas County

Wisconsin

Aquinas Middle School
315 South 11th Street
La Crosse, WI 54601-4763
Phone: (608) 784-0156
Principal: Mrs. Patricia Gallagher-Kosmatka
School District: Aquinas Catholic Schools

Country Meadows Elementary School
S75W16399 Hilltop Drive
Muskego, WI 53150-8849
Phone: (262) 971-1815
Principal: Mr. Gary Goelz
School District: Muskego Norway School District

Grafton Elementary School
1800 Washington Street
Grafton, WI 53024-2100
Phone: (262) 376-5700
Principal: Mr. Jeffrey Martyka
School District: Grafton

Kohler High School
333 Upper Road
Kohler, WI 53044-1545
Phone: (920) 803-7201
Principal: Ms. Quynh Trueblood
School District: Kohler

Our Redeemer Lutheran School
10025 W. North Avenue
Wauwatosa, WI 53226-2501
Phone: (414) 258-4558
Principal: Mrs. Mary Irish
School District: South Wisconsin - LCMS

Ridgeway Elementary School
208 Jarvis Street
Ridgeway, WI 53582-9658
Phone: (608) 924-3461
Principal: Mr. Don Charpentier
School District: Dodgeville

Suamico Elementary School
2153 School Lane
Green Bay, WI 54313-8015
Phone: (920) 662-9800
Principal: Mr. Ryan Welnetz
School District: Howard Suamico

Wyoming

Henry A. Coffeen Elementary School
1053 S. Sheridan Avenue
Sheridan, WY 82801-5637
Phone: (307) 674-9333
Principal: Mrs. Nicole Trahan
School District: Sheridan County
  School District #2

Jackson Hole High School
1910 High School Road
P.O. Box 568
Jackson, WY 83001-0568
Phone: (307) 732-3700
Principal: Dr. M. Scott Crisp
School District: Teton County School District #1

Lovell High School
502 Hampshire Avenue
Lovell, WY 82431-1613
Phone: (307) 548-2256
Principal: Mr. Scott O'Tremba
School District: Big Horn County
  School District #2

www.ingramcontent.com/pod-product-compliance
Lightning Source LLC
Chambersburg PA
CBHW081811280526
45789CB00008B/3089